The End Times

DISCOVERY SERIES BIBLE STUDY
For individuals or groups

Are the statements in the Bible about the future exact enough for us to know what lies ahead? Or are they too vague, too figurative, or too debatable to be of any real value to us today? What difference does it make whether or not we know ahead of time if it's all going to happen anyway? Let's look to the Bible for the answers to these and other important questions about the future.

—*Martin R. De Haan II*
RBC Ministries

This Discovery Series Bible Study is based on
What Can We Know About The Endtimes? (Q1201), one of the popular Discovery Series
booklets from RBC Ministries. Find out more about Discovery Series at
www.discoveryseries.org

DISCOVERY HOUSE
P U B L I S H E R S*

Managing Editor: Dave Branon
Study Guide questions: Sim Kay Tee, Dave Branon
Graphic Design: Steve Gier
Cover Photo: stock.xchng and NASA

ISBN: 978-1-57293-717-8
Printed in the United States of America
First Printing in 2012

Table of Contents

FOREWORD: The End Times. 1

HOW TO USE DISCOVERY SERIES BIBLE STUDIES. 4

FOR DEVOTION AND **MEDITATION:**. 12, 20, 28, 36, 44, 54
Our Daily Bread articles about the end times

1 SETTING THE STAGE   6
EXPECTATIONS / THE COUNTDOWN CONTINUES / KEY TO THE FUTURE
STUDY GUIDE 1   **10**

2 CHRIST'S RETURN IN THE AIR   13
WHAT WILL HAPPEN? / WHEN WILL IT HAPPEN? / JUDGMENT SEAT
STUDY GUIDE 2   **18**

3 THE ANTICHRIST AND UNPARALLELED TROUBLE   21
SATAN'S COUNTERFEIT / TROUBLE ON EARTH / NATIONS / ISRAEL
STUDY GUIDE 3   **26**

4 THE SECOND COMING AND MILLENNIAL REIGN   29
TRIBULATION / CHRIST'S THOUSAND-YEAR REIGN
STUDY GUIDE 4   **34**

5 JUDGMENT FOR UNBELIEVERS/ NEW WORLD   37
REBELLION ABOLISHED / UNBELIEVERS JUDGED / NEW WORLD CREATED
STUDY GUIDE 5   **42**

6 CONSIDERING THE FACTS   45
WHAT WE CAN'T KNOW / TWO PHASES OF CHRIST'S RETURN / WHY STUDY THIS?
STUDY GUIDE 6   **52**

7 FINAL THOUGHTS: WHAT DOES THIS MEAN?   55
A LIFE TURNED AROUND / WHAT DOES THIS MEAN TO ME?

Leader's and User's Guide   58

How To Use
DISCOVERY SERIES BIBLE STUDIES

The Purpose

The Discovery Series Bible Study (DSBS) series provides assistance to pastors and lay leaders in guiding and teaching fellow Christians with lessons adapted from RBC Ministries Discovery Series booklets and supplemented from items taken from the pages of *Our Daily Bread.* The DSBS series uses the inductive study method to help Christians understand the Bible more clearly.

The Format

READ: Each DSBS book is divided into a series of lessons. For each lesson, you will read a few pages that will give you insight into one aspect of the overall study. Included in some studies will be FOCAL POINT and TIME OUT FOR THEOLOGY segments to help you think through the material. These can be used as discussion starters for group sessions.

RESPOND: At the end of the reading is a two-page STUDY GUIDE to help participants respond to and reflect on the subject. If you are the leader of a group study, ask each member to preview the STUDY GUIDE before the group gets together. Don't feel that you have to work your way through each question in the STUDY GUIDE; let the interest level of the participants dictate the flow of the discussion. The questions are designed for either group or individual study. Here are the parts of that guide:

MEMORY VERSE: A short Scripture passage that focuses your thinking on the biblical truth at hand and can be used for memorization. You might suggest memorization as a part of each meeting.

WARMING UP: A general interest question that can foster discussion (group) or contemplation (individual).

THINKING THROUGH: Questions that will help a group or a student interact with the reading. These questions help drive home the critical concepts of the book.

DIGGING IN: An inductive study of a related passage of Scripture, reminding the group or the student of the importance of Scripture as the final authority.

GOING FURTHER: A two-part wrap-up of the response: REFER suggests ways to compare the ideas of the lesson with teachings in other parts of the Bible. REFLECT challenges the group or the learner to apply the teaching in real life.

OUR DAILY BREAD: After each STUDY GUIDE session will be an *Our Daily Bread* article that relates to the topic. You can use this for further reflection or for an introduction to a time of prayer.

Go to the Leader's and User's Guide on page 58 for further suggestions about using this Discovery Series Bible Study.

1

Setting the Stage

Contemplate Expectations

- *A woman in her ninth month of pregnancy.*
- *A teenager before his first date.*
- *A patient who has been told he has cancer.*

- *A college student the week before final exams.*
- *A man and woman as they say, "I do."*
- *A criminal awaiting the judge's sentence.*

Do your expectations turn out to be naively optimistic, unduly pessimistic, or surprisingly realistic? In most cases, what makes the difference is whether you acted on the basis of specific knowledge or on unfounded feelings.

Opinions about the future follow the same pattern. To avoid being victimized by false hopes or unrealistic fears, we need to search out reliable information and live by it.

Many find it hard to know whom to believe. Some predict a nuclear holocaust. Others speak ominously of mass starvation. Many economists are forecasting a worldwide financial collapse. Still others see a peaceful utopia just ahead.

Here are a few excerpts from actual conversations with people who expressed their hopes and fears about the end times.

FOCAL POINT

"For the Christian who enters into the wonder of salvation as he walks and has intimate fellowship with Him, it is only natural to long to see Christ face to face."
—John F. Walvoord
What We Believe

• "I heard some guy on TV talk about the book of Revelation, and it really spooked me."

• "I believe that I will see the end of the earth in my lifetime."

• "I don't see why Jesus would have to come back. If He was the Messiah, He would have done it right then."

• "If the judgment day comes, then I'm going to hell. I enjoy doing the things I'm doing wrong."

• "It's kind of scary to think that the world is going to come to an end someday, but if I have faith there is nothing to be afraid of."

• "I think everybody has the same destiny."

• "The future kind of scares me. I'm afraid of World War III and things like that."

• "I think God cares, but I don't think He's controlling things. I think He sees what happens, and He hopes for the best."

• "I believe that God controls the future and that Jesus Christ will return just as He promised. I believe in an actual heaven and hell."

Who's right? Which expectations are in line with what we can know for sure? In this study, we will be looking to the Bible for answers to our questions about the end times.

The Countdown Continues

No amount of effort can stop the clock of history. No mortal, no matter how influential, wealthy, or well-known, can break the tyranny of time. Every day that passes, every flash of a digital crystal brings us closer to the dramatic events predicted in the Bible. We can prepare for the inevitable. We can put time to good use. But we cannot stop it. Not for a moment.

That can be an unsettling thought. The prophetic passages of the Bible are filled with frightening scenes and complicated symbols. There are predictions of the sun going dark and the moon turning to blood. Four terrible horsemen are pictured as riding forth over the earth bringing war, famine, disease, and death. A blasphemous beast will rise out of the sea to shake his fist in the face of God and to bring untold suffering to God's children. A final, cataclysmic war will be fought, and blood will flow five feet deep in a valley two hundred miles long. Finally, peace will settle over the earth like the warm, benevolent sunshine of spring.

These are frightening, confusing images. And when we read about

■ FOCAL POINT

"No one who takes the Bible seriously can doubt the return of the Lord Jesus Christ. His second coming is mentioned 240 times in the New Testament."

—Dr. M. R. De Haan

Signs of the Times

prophecy, we come across technical terms such as the great tribulation, the abomination of desolation, the return of Jesus Christ, the great white throne judgment, and the lake of fire.

What's ahead? How much can we know about the end times? Well, not everything, certainly. But the Bible does give us much information. In the pages that follow, we will identify and explain the seven major events of the end times.

 # Christ: Key To The Future

Christ is the center of God's plan for the end times.

1. Return In The Air: Christ comes back for His own.

2. Rise Of The Antichrist: Christ is challenged.

3. Unparalleled Trouble: Christ troubles the nations and Israel.

4. Return To The Earth: Christ comes to rescue and judge Israel, and to judge the nations.

5. Thousand-Year Reign: Christ rules the world from an earthly throne.

6. Final Judgment: Christ defeats His enemies and judges unbelievers.

7. New World: Christ creates a new heaven and a new earth.

Setting the Stage

To understand an overview of the prophetic picture.

MEMORY VERSE
Hebrews 9:28—

"Christ was offered once to bear the sins of many. To those who eagerly wait for Him He will appear a second time, apart from sin, for salvation."

Warming Up

Everyone tends to be curious and fascinated about future events. Why do you think this is true? Where do people usually turn to find out about the future?

Thinking Through

1. What does the term *end time* make you think about? Why should Christians be concerned about end-time events? What difference does it make whether or not we know about end-time events?

2. Several opinions expressing people's hopes and fears about the end times are listed on pages 7–8. What other opinions have you heard, and how did you respond to them?

3. Of the seven stages of future events listed on page 9, which ones do you find most confusing? Most frightening? Most comforting? In each case, why?

Going Further

Refer

In what ways is Christ the "key to the future"? (See Daniel 7:13–14; Matthew 24:30–31; 25:31–34; John 14:3,6; Revelation 1:17–18.)

Why must Christ come to earth a second time? (See Matthew 25:31–34; Mark 13:31; Luke 21:27–28; Acts 1:11; Hebrews 9:28.)

1. What circumstances surrounded Jesus' declaration of comfort in these verses? Where and when did He say these words, and how did that context help us to understand His words?

[1] "Let not your heart be troubled; you believe in God, believe also in Me. [2] In My Father's house are many mansions; if it were not so, I would have told you. I go to prepare a place for you. [3] And if I go and prepare a place for you, I will come again and receive you to Myself; that where I am, there you may be also."

2. Why does Jesus connect our present peace of mind to His promises about future events?

3. Notice how many times Jesus uses the personal pronoun "I." How are these promises linked to what Christ himself will accomplish? Why is His credibility important to our present peace of mind and expectations for the future?

Prayer Time ▶

Use the *Our Daily Bread* article on the next page as a guide for a devotional and meditation time relating to the end times.

Reflect

In John 14:1–3, notice how many times Jesus uses the word *you* to personalize His promises. To what extent do you experience this peace that He has promised? Have you embraced these words of promise in your own heart? If not, will you now?

11

Surrendered Crowns

During her reign, Queen Victoria listened to the palace chaplain preach a sermon on the significance of the second coming of Christ. Those near the royal box noticed that the queen was shaking, her lips were quivering, and her eyes were filled with tears. When the service ended, she asked to see the chaplain alone. Observing her emotion, he asked why she was so moved, and she replied, "Because of what you said about the coming again of the world's rightful King. I could wish still to be here when He returns that I might lay my crown at His blessed feet!"

In the Bible there are many divinely given incentives for faithful service that involve both our acts and our motives. Someday "each one will receive his own reward according to his own labor" (1 Corinthians 3:8). These rewards, designated as "crowns" in the New Testament, can be earned by those who have received the gift of eternal life. Perhaps you say, "O, I would never expect to be rewarded for what I do for Christ." Have you considered what you will do with any crown you receive on that day? There will be no trophy cases in Glory— no gloating over earthly accomplishments! "The Lamb is all the glory in Immanuel's land!" There redeemed, transformed sinners will have the transcendent joy of casting their crowns before the Throne, saying, "You are worthy, O Lord, to receive glory and honor and power" (Revelation 4:11).

—*Paul Van Gorder*

REVELATION 4:10–11—

The twenty-four elders fall down before Him . . . and cast their crowns before the throne.

■ Read today's *Our Daily Bread* at **www.rbc.org/odb**

2

Christ's Return in the Air

Because Christ can be trusted, we know that He will keep His promise to return for His own. He promised His disciples: "I go to prepare a place for you. And if I go and prepare a place for you, I will come again and receive you to Myself; that where I am, there you may be also" (John 14:2–3).

What Will Happen?

This event is described in 1 Thessalonians 4:

> *The Lord Himself will descend from heaven with a shout,*
> *with the voice of an archangel, and with the trumpet of God.*
> *And the dead in Christ will rise first. Then we who are alive and*
> *remain shall be caught up together with them in the clouds to*
> *meet the Lord in the air (vv. 16–17).*

At a predetermined time, the Son of God will leave the Father's side and descend toward earth. As He does, three mighty sounds will echo across the halls of heaven and sweep over the earth: a shout, the voice of an archangel, and a blast from the trumpet of God. When these sounds are heard, all believers since the time of Christ will be resurrected. The bodies of the Christians who have died will arise, be transformed, be reunited with their souls, and be taken to Christ's side in the air. Then every living Christian will be removed from the earth, "caught up" to join with the resurrected believers for a great and glorious meeting in the air. Christ will take them to be with himself, and they will "always be with the Lord" (v. 17).

This is also in view in 1 Corinthians 15:51–52, where Paul wrote:

> *We shall not all sleep, but we shall all be changed—in a moment, in the*
> *twinkling of an eye, at the last trumpet. For the trumpet will sound, and the*
> *dead will be raised incorruptible, and we shall be changed.*

In a moment of time the earth will be emptied of Christians.

When Will It Happen?

No one really knows when this event will occur. The time is not spelled out in prophecy. We are told instead to maintain an attitude and condition of readiness, for Christ said:

> *Therefore you also be ready, for the Son of Man is coming at an hour you do not expect (Matthew 24:44).*

Christ taught this attitude of watchfulness in two similar parables recorded in Luke 12. In the first parable (vv. 35–40), He likened His coming to the return of the master of the house from a wedding. In the second (vv. 42–48), a man has left his household affairs in the hands of a servant.

The key element in both parables is that the day of the master's return could not be known. Because of that, the servants were to maintain constant readiness. The same is true of us as we wait for Christ's return.

This could occur at any moment. That's what the word *imminent* means. But that does not necessarily mean His return will occur soon. Yes, it's imminent—it could take place before you take your next breath, but it is not necessarily immediate. The Lord could delay His return another few hundred years.

We believe that this event will be the first of the end-time events. It is referred to as "the rapture of the church." The word *rapture* comes from the Latin word *rapere,* which literally means "to seize" or "to catch away." For an explanation of why we believe that the rapture is separate from the second coming of Christ to the earth, see pages 47–49.

The Judgment Seat Of Christ

Those who are taken from the earth will meet Christ in the clouds and go to be with Him. Then they will stand before the Lord in judgment. This event is called the judgment seat of Christ. Paul foresaw it when he wrote:

We must all appear before the judgment seat of Christ, that each one may receive the things done in the body, according to what he has done, whether good or bad (2 Corinthians 5:10).

The issue for those at the judgment seat of Christ will not be salvation. They are all God's children—forgiven and adopted on the basis of their acceptance of Christ. The purpose is to determine the degree of reward they receive. They will be called into account and receive what is due them (2 Corinthians 5:10). The primary issue will be faithfulness (1 Corinthians

■ FOCAL POINT

"Moreover it is required in stewards that one be found faithful. But with me it is a very small thing that I should be judged by your or by a human court. In fact, I do not even judge myself. For I know of nothing against myself, yet I am not justified by this; but He who judges me is the Lord. Therefore judge nothing before the time, until the Lord comes, who will both bring to light the hidden things of darkness and reveal the counsels of the hearts. Then each one's praise will come from God."

—1 Corinthians 4:2–5

4:2, 4). This is emphasized in three of our Lord's parables: the worker in the vineyard (Matthew 20:1–16), the talents (Matthew 25:14–30), and the ten minas (Luke 19:11–27).

Some will receive reward at the judgment seat of Christ; others will suffer loss (1 Corinthians 3:11–15). We are not told just what this will involve. There will be no punishment, for Jesus Christ bore all the penalty for our sin on the cross. We may be shown our shortcomings and failures. We may be reminded of our selfishness and of the sins we did not confess. The "loss" we suffer will be in the receiving of less reward than we could have received.

2 Christ's Return in the Air

STUDY GUIDE
read pages 13–17

To understand the Bible's teachings about the rapture and the judgment seat of Christ.

MEMORY VERSE
1 Corinthians 15:51–52—
"Behold, I tell you a mystery: We shall not all sleep, but we shall all be changed—in a moment, in the twinkling of an eye, at the last trumpet."

Warming Up

What would you do if you awoke one morning to find that a loved one in your family had disappeared— suddenly and unexpectedly—without a trace?

Thinking Through

1. On page 14, we are told of three mighty sounds that will sweep the earth at Christ's return for His children. What are they, and what do you think is their significance?

2. What is the key element of the two parables of watchfulness discussed on page 15? How can that key element affect the way we live for Christ each day?

3. How does the judgment seat of Christ fit into the prophetic scheme? (pp. 16–17). What will the primary issue of that judgment be? What is meant by "rewards" and "loss" at this judgment? (See also 1 Corinthians 3:11–15; 9:24–27.)

Going Further

Refer

Using a concordance, study Bible, Bible dictionary, or reputable website, find Bible passages that speak about the different kinds of rewards that a Christian can expect to receive at the judgment seat of Christ. (Hint: Look for keywords like *crown* or *reward*.)

1. The context of the passage is that Paul is answering a question posed by believers who had seen loved ones taken in death. How did these words of Christ's return help them to fulfill the challenge of verse 18?

[16] The Lord Himself will descend from heaven with a shout, with the voice of an archangel, and with the trumpet of God. And the dead in Christ will rise first. [17] Then we who are alive and remain shall be caught up together with them in the clouds to meet the Lord in the air. And thus we shall always be with the Lord. [18] Therefore comfort one another with these words.

2. The phrase "we who are alive" reveals Paul's conviction about the imminence of Christ's return. What was that conviction, and why should we share it today?

3. Paul said to "comfort one another with these words" (v. 18). How does the promise of the rapture comfort you? What hope does the rapture hold for those whose Christian loved ones have already died?

Prayer Time ▶

Use the *Our Daily Bread* article on the next page as a guide for a devotional and meditation time relating to the end times.

Reflect

Are you ready at this moment to appear before Christ's judgment seat? What do you think the Lord would say to you? (See Matthew 25:21, 26.) What rewards do you think you would receive from Him?

What changes in your life are needed so that you will not be ashamed to stand before Christ at His judgment seat? (See Matthew 24:36-46.)

Working Is Waiting

I n 1975, forty people, all members of the same clan, began a vigil in Grannis, Arkansas. They were looking for the second coming of Jesus. Family members quit their jobs and stopped paying their bills. Six of the children dropped out of school. The long wait ended, however, when a judge ordered the youngsters back to classes, and the group was evicted from the house in which they were all staying. When interviewed, one of them said, "We'd do it all over again if that's what we thought we should do. We still think we're right. We know the end is near."

This incident raises two vital questions. Does Christ's return make a significant difference in our lives? While those people were wrong in abdicating their duty, they did take seriously Jesus' words to watch. The other question is this: How are we to wait for that great event? By shelving our responsibilities and doing nothing? No indeed! Paul admonished the believers at Thessalonica to work with their hands and live honestly before the world.

The truth of Jesus' second coming is a life-changing reality. If we are unaffected by it, we're being untrue to Christ's command. However, it should never cause us to become uninvolved in life. To avoid this, let's remind ourselves each morning that this could be the day when the trumpet will sound while giving ourselves completely to our tasks. The best way to be found waiting is to be found working.

—*Dennis De Haan*

1 THESSALONIANS 4:11—

Mind your own business, . . . work with your own hands.

● Read today's *Our Daily Bread* at **www.rbc.org/odb**

3

The Antichrist and Unparalleled Trouble

The Rise of Satan's Counterfeit

Accroding to Bible prophecy, the next event on the end-time calendar after the rapture and the judgment seat is the rise of a false christ to world prominence. He is called the Antichrist.

The apostle John said that many false christs would appear (1 John 2:18; 4:3). Claiming to be the Messiah, they will seek and attract many people. Some had already appeared while John was still alive. One day, however, the ultimate imposter will come. He will gather a huge following.

He will deceive Israel into signing a false peace treaty (Daniel 9:27). And he will be the cause of untold suffering in the world, especially for the saints.

Here is what the Bible tells us about Antichrist:

- He will receive power from Satan (Revelation 13:2).
- He will receive his throne from Satan (Revelation 13:2).
- He will receive his authority from Satan (Revelation 13:2).
- He will be a ruler (Revelation 6:2).
- His purpose will be conquest (Revelation 6:2).
- He will be guilty of terrible blasphemy (Revelation 13:5).
- He will make a peace treaty with Israel and then cruelly break it (Daniel 9:27).
- He will put himself above everything and everyone (Daniel 11:37).
- He will proclaim himself to be God (2 Thessalonians 2:4).
- He will stage a miraculous "resurrection" (Revelation 13:3).
- He will make war with the saints (Revelation 13:7).
- He will have authority over the nations (Revelation 13:7).
- His number is 666 (Revelation 13:18).
- He will kill millions of believers (Revelation 6:9–11; 7:9–17).
- A false prophet will serve him (Revelation 19:20).
- He will demand that his image be worshiped (Revelation 13:14).

The Antichrist is Satan's counterfeit. As Jesus Christ was sent by the Father, so this false christ will be sent by Satan. The Antichrist is given various descriptive names in the Bible. For example, he is referred to as:

- The Little Horn (Daniel 7:7–28).
- The King of Fierce Countenance (Daniel 8:23–25).
- The Prince Who Is to Come (Daniel 9:26–27).
- The Willful King (Daniel 11:16, 36–38).
- The Man of Sin (2 Thessalonians 2:3–4).
- The Son of Perdition (2 Thessalonians 2:3–4).
- The Beast (Revelation 13:1–10).

The Earth Will Experience Unparalleled Trouble

When the Antichrist is revealed, the stage will be set for the terrible events of the tribulation. After this satanically empowered leader rises to prominence, the most distressing period of all history will follow. For three and a half years the Antichrist will conduct a reign of terror, bringing death to multitudes, both Jew and Gentile. But in addition to this reign of terror, the earth will experience unparalleled trouble as God's wrath is poured out on all mankind (Isaiah 13:6–11).

The Nations Troubled

The nations will not go unpunished by the hand of God. They will live to hate the day they cast their lot with God's archenemy. For generations their leaders will have rejected God and mocked His Son. A just punishment will befall them in the seven-year period called "the tribulation." Two sections of the New Testament describe the events of these seven years: Matthew 24 and Revelation 6–16. These prophetic details indicate how mankind will suffer during this frightening time:

MATTHEW 24

- false christs
- wars
- rumors of war
- nation against nation
- famines
- earthquakes
- killing
- betrayal
- flight
- pestilences

The Seals (Revelation 6)

1. Antichrist
2. war
3. famine
4. death
5. martyrdom
6. global destruction
7. the trumpets begin

The Trumpets (Revelation 8–9)

1. vegetation destroyed
2. death at sea
3. fresh water poisoned
4. the heavens struck
5. terrible locusts
6. death by demons
7. the bowl judgments begin

The Bowls (Revelation 15–16)

1. ugly sores
2. death of marine life
3. fresh water contaminated
4. unbearable heat
5. darkness and pain
6. demonic hordes
7. earthquake and hail

The suffering and death that will fall on the nations during the tribulation is indescribably horrible. Millions will die in the terrible outpouring of God's wrath. Yet the majority will not repent. Though they will gnaw their tongues in agony (Revelation 16:10), they will continue to curse the God of heaven and refuse to trust in Him (vv. 10–11). There will be a large number multitude of Gentiles, however, who will turn to God during the tribulation. John refers to them as "a great multitude . . . of all nations, tribes, peoples, and tongues" (Revelation 7:9).

Israel Troubled

There are actually two purposes for the seven years of tribulation. The first, as we have already seen, is the punishment of the nations. A second is to bring Israel to the place where she can be restored to the position of spiritual favor she once held in God's eyes. Israel will suffer with the nations—only more intensely. This is "the time of Jacob's trouble" prophesied by Jeremiah:

Alas! For that day is great, so that none is like it; and it is the time of Jacob's trouble, but he shall be saved out of it (Jeremiah 30:7).

The tribulation will be a time of suffering and death for all mankind. But the Jews will be the hardest hit by the terror of those awful days. Zechariah predicted that two-thirds of all Jews on earth will die during the tribulation (13:8–9). But the suffering will bring Israel to repentance.

The prophet Ezekiel described Israel's conversion with these beautiful words:

I will take you from among the nations, gather you out of all countries, and bring you into your own land. Then I will sprinkle clean water on you, and you shall be clean; I will cleanse you from all your filthiness and from all your idols. I will give you a new heart and put a new spirit within you; I will take the heart of stone out of your flesh and give you a heart of flesh. I will put My Spirit within you and cause you to walk in My statutes, and you will keep My judgments and do them. Then you shall dwell in the land that I gave to your fathers; you shall be My people, and I will be your God (Ezekiel 36:24–28).

Biblical descriptions of Israel's restoration are also given in Ezekiel 37 (the valley of dry bones) and Zechariah 12:10–11.

The spiritual restoration of Israel as a nation will take place at the return of Jesus Christ to earth at the end of the tribulation. When He returns to rescue the people of Israel from being annihilated by the Antichrist, they will nationally accept Him as their Messiah and Savior, even though individually a large number of Jews will already have been converted (Revelation 7:1–8).

After hundreds of generations of hardhearted disbelief, the people of Israel will trust in Jesus Christ as their true Messiah. In terrible agony, inflicted by the Antichrist, they will turn in faith to the Lord Jesus. This brings us to the next event in God's program for the end times: the return of Jesus Christ to earth.

3 The Antichrist and Trouble

STUDY GUIDE

read pages 21–25

MEMORY VERSE

1 John 4:3—

"Every spirit that does not confess that Jesus Christ has come in the flesh is not of God. And this is the spirit of the Antichrist."

To learn more about the person identified as the Antichrist and the seven-year period of tribulation on the earth.

Warming Up

From movies to pulpits to politics, there's been much speculation about the identity of the Antichrist. Why is there so much interest? What world leaders or celebrities in recent memory have been suspected of being the Antichrist? What reasons have been given? _____

Thinking Through

1. On pages 21 and 22, we are told of a significant event involving the Antichrist and his relationship with Israel. What is it, and how would such an event be received in today's world? _____

2. What are the three series of judgments that will trouble the world after Antichrist's appearance? What will be the results of these judgments (p. 24)? _____

3. What is the purpose of the time of trouble for the nation of Israel (pp. 24–25)? Why do you think such suffering is necessary to accomplish this goal? _____

Going Further

Refer

Think about and discuss the emotions that 1 Thessalonians 2:19, which relates directly to 2 Thessalonians 2:1, brings out in you as you think about that future day. _____

What are some of the works of the antichrists that are already seen in the world? (See 1 John 2:18, 22; 4:3; 2 John 1:7.) How do these things affect the life and witness of Christians today? _____

1. Why are the terms "man of sin" and "son of perdition" (v. 3) appropriate for a false Christ sent by Satan?

2. According to verses 5 and 6, the people of Thessalonica knew what was restraining the "man of sin." What do you think is the identity of the restrainer mentioned in verse 7? How is this restraining being accomplished? What did Paul mean when he said the restrainer would be "taken out of the way" (v. 7)?

3. What is the fate awaiting the Antichrist or "lawless one" (v. 8)? How does the fact that his fate is already predetermined and sealed give us comfort or assurance?

3 Let no one deceive you by any means; for that Day will not come unless the falling away comes first, and the man of sin is revealed, the son of perdition, 4 who opposes and exalts himself above all that is called God or that is worshiped, so that he sits as God in the temple of God, showing himself that he is God.

5 Do you not remember that when I was still with you I told you these things? 6 And now you know what is restraining, that he may be revealed in his own time. 7 For the mystery of lawlessness is already at work; only He who now restrains will do so until He is taken out of the way. 8 And then the lawless one will be revealed, whom the Lord will consume with the breath of His mouth and destroy with the brightness of His coming.

Prayer Time ▶

Use the *Our Daily Bread* article on the next page as a guide for a devotional and meditation time relating to the end times.

Reflect

A believer considering the terrors of the tribulation and the Antichrist should have at least two responses: thankfulness for salvation and concern for the lost who will go through this terrible time on the earth. In what ways does knowledge of the end times help us to share Christ with those who don't know Him?

Delusions

People sometimes suffer from delusions that are sad but not dangerous. For instance, we've all heard of those who claim to be Napoleon or some other historical figure. We feel sorry for such people, even though their misconceptions may be harmless. Sometimes, however, mistaken convictions can be dangerous. For example, Hitler saw himself as the head of a super race, and he killed millions of innocent people because of this twisted thinking. The apostle Paul says the time is coming when the Antichrist, someone far worse than Hitler, will come with "signs and lying wonders" (2 Thessalonians 2:8–9). He will deceive many into thinking that he is Jesus. They will believe him because they are people who "did not receive the love of the truth" (v. 10).

Experience confirms that people who continually reject the truth will eventually become so deluded that they'll believe something they once knew to be untrue. That was the case with many Germans who at first had strong misgivings about Hitler. But they kept listening to him and became so deluded that they eventually supported him.

Are you listening to people who take sin lightly or proclaim a way of salvation different from what the Bible teaches? Beware! If you keep listening, you may be deceived into believing a lie. Study the Bible and obey the truth. Don't risk being deluded!

—*Herb Vander Lugt*

2 THESSALONIANS 2:10–11—

They did not receive the love of the truth, that they might be saved. And for this reason God will send them strong delusion, that they should believe the lie.

■ Read today's *Our Daily Bread* at **www.rbc.org/odb**

4

The Second Coming and Millennnial Reign

Christ Will Return To The Earth

As the tribulation draws to a close, the earth will be in turmoil. Millions will have died in war or its aftermath. The Antichrist's hatred of God will focus on the Jews as the seven years reach their conclusion.

Opposed from the north and east (Daniel 11:44–45), the Antichrist will march his armies into Palestine in preparation for a vast military showdown. Evil spirits will draw the nations together for a final battle on the plains of Megiddo (Revelation 16:12–16).

The armies assembled in Palestine will be made up of bloodthirsty men who have resisted God throughout the tribulation. Both sides—the Antichrist and his opponents—will hate the people of God. They will engage in a fierce battle at Armageddon. The fighting will reach Jerusalem, and the Jews living there will suffer horribly (Zechariah 14:1–2). A sense of despair will sweep over them as both armies attack them.

Suddenly, when all seems hopeless, the scene will change. Jesus Christ will appear in all His glory and descend to the Mount of Olives. When His

■ FOCAL POINT

"Now I saw heaven opened, and behold, a white horse. And He who sat on him was called Faithful and True, and in righteousness He judges and makes war. His eyes were like a flame of fire, and on His head were many crowns. He had a name written that no one knew except Himself."

—Revelation 19:11–12

feet touch it, the mountain will split in half, forming a vast new valley stretching from the Jordan River to the Mediterranean Sea (14:3–9). The Jewish believers will be given superhuman strength to fight the Lord's enemies (12:6–9), God will send a plague on the enemy soldiers and their animals (14:12, 15), and panic will grip the foreign troops, causing them to attack one another (14:13).

In Revelation 19:11–21, the apostle John provides us with a beautiful portrait of Christ's second coming. He is depicted astride a white horse, His eyes blazing. The Antichrist will rally the armies of earth to attack Him, but they will be crushed in defeat. Israel will be rescued. The armed hordes of earth will be slain. The Antichrist and his cohort will be thrown into the lake of fire. Satan himself will be bound. And the victorious Christ will prepare to ascend His throne in Jerusalem to rule in peace for one thousand years.

 ## Those Who Survive The Tribulation

Jesus Christ will hold two special judgments at the close of the tribulation. The first will be for the Jews who survive those terrible days. The prophet Ezekiel described the Lord Jesus as a shepherd standing at the door of a sheepfold. The Jews who have trusted Him will be received into His kingdom; those who rejected Him will not (Ezekiel 20:33–44).

A similar judgment will be held for the Gentiles who live through the tribulation. Again, a shepherd metaphor is used to describe Christ. He is pictured as separating the sheep from the goats (Matthew 25:31–46). Believers in Christ (the sheep) will be allowed to enter the millennial kingdom; unbelievers (the goats) will die and await the great white throne judgment (see p. 29).

 ## Christ Will Rule The Earth For One Thousand Years

The battle is over. The armed hordes of the earth have been defeated. Just when all seemed lost, Jesus Christ appeared in glory, leading His armies to earth. Before the day ended, the Battle of Armageddon had been won by Him. But the earth is in ruins. Death and destruction lie everywhere. What will happen?

Rather than returning to His Father in heaven, Jesus Christ will erect His throne in Jerusalem, establish it as His capital city, reinstate the Jews as His people, and rule over the entire earth in a one thousand-year reign of peace, prosperity, and righteousness, which we call the millennium (Revelation 20:4–6).

The Old Testament prophecies are filled with details about the new government Christ will establish when He returns. Here is what life will be like when the Lord Jesus rules the world:

1. CHRIST WILL BE KING

- The Branch of David will rule (Jeremiah 23:5).
- Christ will fulfill His prophesied rule (Luke 1:32–33).
- The believers of the church age will reign with Christ (Revelation 20:4, 6).

2. ISRAEL WILL BE PROMINENT

- Israel will be the favored nation (Isaiah 2:1–3).
- Jerusalem will be the capital city (Isaiah 60:10–14).
- David's throne will be reestablished (Luke 1:32).

3. CHRIST'S RULE WILL REFLECT HIS CHARACTER

- Justice for everyone (Isaiah 2:4).
- All will prosper (Micah 4:4).
- He will reign in righteousness (Jeremiah 23:5).
- The earth will be at peace (Zechariah 8:4–5).
- People will be safe (Jeremiah 23:5–6).

4. THE NATURAL WORLD WILL BE TRANSFORMED

- The climate will be ideal (Isaiah 30:23–26).
- Wild animals will be tame (Isaiah 11:6–8).
- Fishing will be great (Ezekiel 47:9–10).
- People will have good health (Isaiah 35:5–6).

• Life will be lengthened (Isaiah 65:19–20, 22).

• Trees will provide food and medicine (Ezekiel 47:12).

5. GOD WILL BE WORSHIPED

• His name will be known throughout the world (Malachi 1:11).

• The temple at Jerusalem will be the center of worship (Ezekiel 40–48).

• Representatives will come from everywhere (Zechariah 14:16).

• All mankind will come (Isaiah 66:23).

• The Jews will lead in worship (Isaiah 60:10–14).

When Christ rules in the millennial kingdom, His love, justice, mercy, righteousness, and peace will be found throughout the earth. Since people reflect their ruler, the people of the kingdom will reflect the characteristics of their King. During this golden age, the earth will be what God intended it to be.

The Second Coming...

STUDY GUIDE

read pages 29–33

MEMORY VERSE

Matthew 25:31—
"When the Son of Man comes in His glory, and all the holy angels with Him, then He will sit on the throne of His glory."

To consider the return of Christ to the earth and His resulting rule in power and glory for one thousand years.

Warming Up

What images does the word *Armageddon* conjure up in your mind? Do you think Armageddon will be World War III? Why or why not?

Thinking Through

1. Jesus will come to rescue Israel from the armies of the world at the Battle of Armageddon (p. 30). The word *Armageddon* is often used to refer to the end of the world, but what's the biblical view of that great battle?

2. What two special judgments follow the close of the tribulation (p. 31)? Who is involved in those judgments? How do they differ from the judgment seat of Christ?

3. What are the five main characteristics of the millennium, the earthly kingdom of Christ (pp. 32–33)? Why can these things happen only when Christ personally reigns on earth?

Going Further

Refer

Using whatever resources you have handy, list some other Scripture passages that refer to the millennial rule of Christ.

1. What is the fate awaiting Satan (vv. 1–3)? Why is he bound for one thousand years? What would life be like without Satan's influence on the earth?

2. How many times is one thousand years referred to in this text? Is it more reasonable to think that this is a symbolic or a literal period of time? Why?

4 And I saw thrones, and they sat on them, and judgment was committed to them. Then I saw the souls of those who had been beheaded for their witness to Jesus and for the word of God, who had not worshiped the beast or his image, and had not received his mark on their foreheads or on their hands. And they lived and reigned with Christ for a thousand years. 5 But the rest of the dead did not live again until the thousand years were finished. This is the first resurrection. 6 Blessed and holy is he who has part in the first resurrection. Over such the second death has no power, but they shall be priests of God and of Christ, and shall reign with Him a thousand years.

3. According to verses 4–6, who will reign with Christ during His millennial kingdom? Who else will share in that reign? (See 1 Corinthians 6:2; 2 Timothy 2:12; Revelation 1:6; 5:10.)

Prayer Time ⫸

Use the *Our Daily Bread* article on the next page as a guide for a devotional and meditation time relating to the end times.

Reflect

People of every generation have longed to see this world rescued from conflict and strife, and brought into a condition of peace and harmony. Although this will happen perfectly when Christ rules in His kingdom, what can we do now to be peacemakers in our strife-torn world?

Does the fact that you will sit on a throne and reign with Christ threaten or encourage you? Why is it possible for us to share in this privilege?

Jesus Is Coming

n *National Geographic* magazine I read a fascinating article entitled "A Pacific Island Awaits Its Messiah." The "christ" referred to is not the Lord Jesus, but a legendary figure called John Frum. The author, Dr. Kal Muller, pointed out that the islanders think this person will be either a "beneficent spirit," a "god come to earth," or "king of America." The third description has its origin in the fact that US troops occupied the area during World War II, and their presence was accompanied by many material benefits. The people concluded that John Frum had arrived.

Although they experienced keen disappointment when the soldiers left, their hopes did not die. They frequently march with bamboo "rifles" slung over their shoulders and the letters USA painted on their bodies. They are still looking for their messiah, who they think will usher in "a prosperous, work-free millennium" of unlimited earthly goods.

We believers in the Bible are also looking for a coming King. Our hope, however, is grounded upon much more than the imaginations of men who long for physical luxury. It is based upon a "more sure word of prophecy" (2 Peter 1:19). The same blessed Savior who came in the flesh nearly 2,000 years ago, died on the cross, arose from the dead, and showed himself alive "by many infallible proofs" (Acts 1:3) will one day return just as He promised. Our Messiah is no legend; He is the Lord Jesus who lives in heaven. So, keep looking up; for He IS coming again! —*Richard De Haan*

REVELATION 22:20—

He who testifies to these things says, "Surely I am coming quickly."

■ Read today's *Our Daily Bread* at **www.rbc.org/odb**

36

5

Judgment for Unbelievers; A New World

At the end of the one thousand-year reign of Christ on the earth, Satan, who had been locked up during this time, will be released. Immediately gathering a gigantic army of unbelievers together, Satan will lead them in battle against the Lord. This will be Satan's final act of rebellion.

All Rebellion Abolished

John's description is in Revelation 20:7–10.

> *When the thousand years have expired, Satan will be released from his prison and will go out to deceive the nations which are in the four*

corners of the earth, Gog and Magog, to gather them together to battle, whose number is as the sand of the sea. They went up on the breadth of the earth and surrounded the camp of the saints and the beloved city. And fire came down from God out of heaven and devoured them. The devil, who deceived them, was cast into the lake of fire and brimstone where the beast and the false prophet are. And they will be tormented day and night forever and ever.

It had all begun sometime in eternity past, when Lucifer had looked with a jealous eye at the throne of God. In pride he led a rebellion of angels against God and was cast out of heaven (Isaiah 14:12–14; Ezekiel 28:12–15). From the time of his deception in the garden of Eden until he was cast into the bottomless pit, he has brought immeasurable suffering to mankind. Now, after one thousand years of confinement, his hatred of God has intensified. He makes one last, desperate attempt to dethrone the Lord. But in spite of all of his power, his fate will be the same as his wicked underlings, the Antichrist and the False Prophet—everlasting torment in hell.

All Unbelievers Judged

When Satan's last rebellion is smashed, it will be time for the final judgment. A new heaven and a new earth will soon be appearing, and the last details of earth-business must be taken care of. This judgment will occur at the great white throne of God (Revelation 20:11–15).

We are told that "the dead, small and great," (v. 12) will stand before the throne. Unbelievers of Old Testament days, the church age, the tribulation, and the millennium will be there as the books are opened. No one will escape, for "the sea . . . and Death and Hades" (v. 13) will give up their inhabitants. The outcome will not be in question. Those who rejected God's offer of salvation in Christ will have sealed their own fate. Their names will not be found in the Lamb's Book of Life. They will be cast into the lake of fire, which is already inhabited by Satan, Antichrist, and the False Prophet. This is the second death—eternal death.

These are not pleasant thoughts. We don't like the idea of eternal suffering. The idea of flames and anguish appalls us. But remember, these are people who intentionally and willfully chose not to trust in Christ. They turned their backs on God's grace, deciding to leave Him out of their lives. It was their own choice.

God is not vengeful and capricious. He does not cause suffering just for the sport of it. His judgment stems from His holiness, and He is absolutely righteous and holy. No one will receive one bit more or less than he deserves, because God can only judge rightly.

When questions of eternal suffering disturb us, let's remember the words of Abraham: "Shall not the Judge of all the earth do right?" (Genesis 18:25). Then, in faith, we can leave it squarely in His hands.

A New World Will Be Created

We come now to the final event on God's prophetic timetable—which, like a commencement, is more of a beginning than an ending. That which begins with the new world will last from that point on—forever. From the ruins of the old heavens and earth, God will bring into existence an eternal new world free from evil, free from deceit, free from all the harmful, debilitating things that have marred the earth since Adam's sin.

The prophetic books are filled with information about the millennial kingdom, but they tell us very little about the new world to come. Most of our information comes from Revelation 21–22. It begins:

I saw a new heaven and a new earth, for the first heaven and the first earth had passed away (21:1).

What will happen to the old world-system? It will be burned to ashes in the aftermath of Satan's final attack (Revelation 20:7–10). Peter described it as follows:

> *The day of the Lord will come as a thief in the night, in which the heavens will pass away with a great noise, and the elements will melt with fervent heat, but the earth and the works that are in it will be burned up (2 Peter 3:10).*

From these charred, smoking ruins, the Creator will bring into existence an eternal home of amazing beauty and grandeur for His own. As we consider the elements of this new world, we will be dazzled by the picture that appears in our minds.

The New Jerusalem

In his vision, John saw the holy city descend from heaven. He described it in Revelation 21 and 22 as follows:

- as beautiful as a bride dressed for her husband (21:2)
- where God dwells with men (21:3)
- immense in size (21:16)
- a jeweled foundation (21:19–20)
- a 216-foot-high wall of jasper (21:17–18)
- 12 gates of pearl, always open (21:21, 25)
- buildings and streets of gold (21:18, 21)
- illuminated by God's glory (21:11, 23)
- a crystal river (22:1)
- trees of life for healing (22:2)
- the throne of God (22:3)

The city is also remarkable for what is not there. The following things will be missing from our heavenly home:

- no sea (21:1)
- no tears (21:4)
- no death (21:4)
- no pain (21:4)
- no sorrow (21:4)
- no temple (21:22)

- no sun (21:23)
- no moon (21:23)
- no impurity (21:27)
- no deceit (21:27)
- no more curse (22:3)
- no night (22:5)

What a wonderful place! There will be no night because our heavenly home will be illuminated by the glory of God, and the Lamb will be its light (21:23; 22:5). There will be no temple because Christ himself will be the temple (21:22). We will reign there forever (22:5). We will see the face of God and bear His name on our foreheads (22:4). We will have access forever to the tree of life (22:2, 14).

With this description of heaven complete, the Bible comes to an end. When we think of the wonders of that home awaiting us, where the Lord himself will dwell with us, we can only say with John, "Even so, come, Lord Jesus!" (Revelation 22:20).

5 Judgment; New World

To recognize the difference between eternal life with Christ and eternal judgment.

MEMORY VERSE
Luke 10:20—
"Nevertheless do not rejoice in this, that the spirits are subject to you, but rather rejoice because your names are written in heaven."

Warming Up

What are some of the popular images you have associated with hell? How accurate do you think those pictures are? What emotions or fears do you have when you think of hell? Why?

Thinking Through

1. On pages 37–39, we are told that at the end of one thousand years of a perfect environment on earth, Satan will lead a final rebellion against God. Why do you think people who have experienced the perfection of the millennial kingdom could so quickly be led into rebellion against a perfect king?

2. What is the great white throne judgment (pp. 38–39)? Why is this judgment necessary? Who is judged, on what basis are they judged, and what is the outcome? How is this judgment different from the judgment seat of Christ?

3. The final portion of Revelation describes the creation of the new heavens and earth. In the list of things that will not be present in this perfect place (pp. 40–41), what is the most comforting to you? Why?

Going Further

Refer

Read Jesus' words in Luke 16:19–31. What insights can you gain about heaven and hell from this passage? What do these verses teach about unbelievers getting a second chance to hear and respond to the gospel after they die?

1. What are some ways the statement "no more sea" in verse 1 distinguishes the eternal state from our present world?

¹ Now I saw a new heaven and a new earth, for the first heaven and the first earth had passed away. Also there was no more sea. ² Then I, John, saw the holy city, New Jerusalem, coming down out of heaven from God, prepared as a bride adorned for her husband. ³ And I heard a loud voice from heaven saying, "Behold, the tabernacle of God is with men, and He will dwell with them, and they shall be His people. God Himself will be with them and be their God. ⁴ And God will wipe away every tear from their eyes; there shall be no more death, nor sorrow, nor crying. There shall be no more pain, for the former things have passed away."

2. Compare verse 3 with Genesis 1–2. How does this wonderful promise restore the relationship with God that was broken in the garden of Eden?

3. According to verse 4, how will God personally care for and comfort His children throughout eternity in the New Jerusalem?

Prayer Time ▶

Use the *Our Daily Bread* article on the next page as a guide for a devotional and meditation time relating to the end times.

Reflect

What effect does the Bible's teaching about heaven and hell have on your motivation to tell people about the forgiveness that is available in Jesus Christ? Ask God to make you more aware of the people around you who need to hear the saving message of the gospel.

Perfect Justice

Rom Eaton spent sixteen years in prison even though he was innocent. At the end of that time behind bars, he made this observation: "I didn't have a dime in my pocket or a friend in the world when they put me on trial for armed robbery. That's why I spent sixteen years in prison for a crime committed by two other men while I was 1,700 miles away. I am free now, completely vindicated. Life played a dirty trick on me in Circuit Court."

REVELATION 20:12—

And I saw the dead, small and great, standing before God... And the dead were judged according to their works.

Such an injustice will never occur in God's "court-room." No one will ever bear the penalty of another person's guilt. No one will be able to claim he or she got a "bad rap" or was the victim of a "dirty trick."

Revelation 20:11–15 previews that day when the unsaved will stand before God, the supreme Judge. The charges made against them will be confirmed by the record of their lives in the books that show their works. The Book of Life will also be opened, and the fact that their names are not found in it will prove that they never trusted in Christ.

Unlike Rom Eaton, who did suffer a cruel injustice, those who appear at the great white throne judgment will agree with the verdict. That's why we must urge all people to accept Christ's offer of pardon now before it's too late. With God there is perfect justice.

—*Paul Van Gorder*

■ Read today's *Our Daily Bread* at **www.rbc.org/odb**

6

Considering the Facts

What We Can't Know About the End Times

No biblical subject brings out the imagination in people more than prophecy. Some people look into the prophetic books and always seem to find things that are sensational. Often their conjectures cannot be supported—either by context or by content. We have been talking in this booklet about end-time events that we know will take place. Let's look now at four things we cannot know about the future but that people often claim to have special knowledge about.

1. THE DATE OF CHRIST'S RETURN

Time and again, self-proclaimed prophets have used Bible statements to support their "findings" that Jesus will return on a certain day or in a certain year. Some of these charlatans have even persuaded their followers to sell their earthly goods, combine their financial resources, and head for the hills to await the Lord's return. But God's Word says clearly, "Therefore you also be ready, for the Son of Man is coming at an hour you do not expect" (Matthew 24:44).

Many Christians fell into the trap of date-setting after Israel became a nation in 1948. They based their conclusion on Matthew 24:32–34, which says that the generation who sees "the fig tree" bud "will by no means pass away till all these things [the events prior to and including Christ's return] take place." Since Israel is pictured as a fig tree in the Old Testament, many believed that the Lord would return within the next generation (40 years). This would date the coming of Christ to the earth sometime before 1988 and the rapture of the church before 1981—obviously not an accurate interpretation of the events.

2. THE IDENTITY OF ANTICHRIST

Whenever a popular world leader with charisma, charm, and intelligence appears on the scene, he is tagged by someone as the Antichrist. In a sense, the people who make this kind of prediction are on the right track. The one who will rise to international prominence during the tribulation will indeed have those characteristics. We have no scriptural basis, however, for knowing beforehand who that man will be. That will become evident only when he is revealed to mankind during the tribulation.

3. THE UNITED STATES IN BIBLICAL PROPHECY

Some Americans find it exciting to think that God may have given the United

States special mention in His Book. They claim, for example, that Revelation 18 reveals the United States as commercial Babylon. Yet nothing in the passage specifically requires that conclusion. The evils it mentions are just as true of almost every other civilization on earth as they are of the United States.

4. SPECIFIC DETAILS

When prophetic experts go beyond what is clearly revealed in the Bible, they are only speculating. In other words, we have no biblical basis for saying that the world will run out of oil, that the United States faces a dictatorship, that paper money will be abolished, or that the number 666 is a computer number. There is a danger in seeing every current event as a fulfillment of prophecy. Details like these are not revealed in the Scriptures.

The Two Phases Of Christ's Return

The end times are more easily understood when a distinction is made between the coming of Christ in the air to remove His church and the coming of Christ to the earth to rescue Israel and set up His kingdom. These are the two phases of Christ's return. This distinction is based on the following evidence:

1. IMMINENCY

The Bible clearly teaches that Christ could return at any time. But it also teaches that certain catastrophic events will take place during the tribulation, prior to His return—putting the Lord's people in a state of readiness and expectation. This problem can be resolved if the coming of Christ is seen in two phases. His coming in the air will be sudden and without warning, but His coming to the earth will be expected by those who are alive during the tribulation and who know the biblical record.

2. ISRAEL AND THE CHURCH

Israel and the church are two distinct entities, with distinct makeup, identity, and destiny. Israel is a nation; the church is made up of people of all nations (including Israel) who put their faith in Christ. Israel is promised prosperity and fulfillment on earth; the church is promised blessings in heavenly places.

3. THE REMOVAL OF THE RESTRAINER

In 2 Thessalonians 2:7 we are told that the way will not be clear for last-day events until a "restrainer" is taken away. It seems very probable that this "restrainer" is the Holy Spirit as He indwells individual members of the church. The removal of these persons, referred to by Christ as the "salt of the earth" and the "light of the world," would clear the way for a worldwide deception.

4. DIFFERING DESCRIPTIONS OF CHRIST'S COMING

First Thessalonians 4:17 pictures Christ coming in the clouds to "catch up" His people to meet with Him in the air, but Zechariah 14:5 and Revelation 19:14 picture Him as coming to the earth with His people.

5. THE CHURCH NOT DESTINED FOR GOD'S WRATH

Revelation 3:10 indicates that the church is not destined for "the hour of trial which shall come upon the whole world." Scripture speaks of "the time of Jacob's trouble" (Jeremiah 30:7) as that future time when Israel will be brought to her knees in preparation for the coming of her Messiah. Israel will suffer before her restoration, but 1 Thessalonians 5:9 indicates that the church will escape that day of God's wrath.

6. THE STATE OF THE KINGDOM INHABITANTS

According to 1 Corinthians 15:51, all the righteous will be changed. And

Since the early days of the church, Christians have been looking forward to the return of Jesus Christ. The apostle Paul, writing to Titus back in the first century, said that we should be "looking for the blessed hope and glorious appearing of the great God and Savior Jesus Christ" (Titus 2:13). One of these days that *blessed hope* is going to become a *blessed reality*.

—Richard De Haan
Jesus is Coming: Perhaps Today!

Matthew 25:41–46 says that all the unrighteous will be sent into everlasting punishment. If there were no distinction between the two phases of Christ's coming, only glorified, transformed believers would be left to inhabit the kingdom. This doesn't seem possible, because children will be born in the millennium (Isaiah 11:6–8). And more important, who does Satan lead in worldwide rebellion against Christ at the end of the millennium if not those unbelievers born during the one thousand years? Initially, only believers will inhabit the kingdom (Ezekiel 20:33–44; Matthew 25:31–46).

Why Study Prophecy?

1. IT PROMOTES LOVE AND RESPECT FOR GOD'S WORD

An understanding of the Scriptures shows that God has fulfilled amazing prophecies in the past. This assures us that He will also fulfill those that predict the end times. Furthermore, a detailed study of the prophetic Scriptures is bound to give us a greater understanding of all Bible truth and a deeper appreciation for God's Word.

2. IT PROMOTES WATCHFULNESS AND PURITY

It will motivate us to be ready for the any-moment return of Jesus Christ. Our Lord himself emphasized this when He referred to Noah, to the faithful servant, to the ten virgins, and to the talents (Matthew 24:36–25:30). The apostle John exhorted us to be faithful, so that when our Lord appears we will be confident and unashamed (1 John 2:28). He went on to say, "Everyone who has this hope in Him purifies himself, just as He is pure" (3:3).

3. IT PROMOTES A PHILOSOPHY OF HISTORY

Even though prophecy does not give us an exactly detailed prewritten history, it does lay out the future course for man and the earth. It tells us that the life God created on earth is worthwhile. It shows that God has specific plans for man and for our planet. He will correct the injustices; He will right the wrongs; He will rid the world of evil. The long, arduous course of human history will climax in a golden age of universal peace, prosperity, and righteousness that will exceed our fondest dreams.

■ FOCAL POINT

God, the architect of the ages, has seen fit to take us into His confidence concerning His plan for the future and has revealed His purpose and program in detail in the Word. A greater body of Scripture is given to prophecy than any other one subject, for approximately one-fourth of the Bible was prophetic at the time it was written. That portion is devoted to the unfolding of God's program.

—J. Dwight Pentecost
Things To Come

Considering the Facts

MEMORY VERSE
Matthew 24:44—

"Therefore you also be ready, for the Son of Man is coming at an hour you do not expect."

To respond to critical issues about the overall scheme of end-time prophecy.

Warming Up

If you knew that Jesus would return at 3:00 p.m. this Friday, what would you be doing between now and then in anticipation of that event? _____

_____

Thinking Through

1. People often claim that they have special knowledge about the end times. What are four things we cannot know about the future (see pp. 46–47)? _____

_____

_____

2. Why is it necessary to see Christ's return in two phases? What evidence supports this view (see pp. 47–49)? What is the meaning of *imminency*? How should a belief in the imminent return of Christ for His church affect the way Christians live?

_____

_____

3. Many people avoid studying prophecy for a variety of reasons, including fear or frustration. What three powerful reasons to study prophecy are given on pages 49–50?

Going Further

Refer

Compare 1 John 3:2 with Romans 8:28–29. What do these passages reveal to be God's purpose for each of His children? How is it achieved? _____

_____

_____

_____

_____

1. The hope of the believer is found in the words of verse 2, "When He is revealed, we shall be like Him, for we shall see Him as He is." How does this parallel 1 Corinthians 15:51–58? What will happen to us at that meeting?

[1] Behold what manner of love the Father has bestowed on us, that we should be called children of God! Therefore the world does not know us, because it did not know Him. [2] Beloved, now we are children of God; and it has not yet been revealed what we shall be, but we know that when He is revealed, we shall be like Him, for we shall see Him as He is. [3] And everyone who has this hope in Him purifies himself, just as He is pure.

2. Contrast the way the world rejects the child of God to the way the Father accepts us (1 John 3:1). How is this acceptance possible, and what are its results? (See Romans 5:1-11.)

3. According to verse 3, what is the result of living in the hope of Christ's return? What is our responsibility in achieving this result? What does this verse, along with 1 John 2:28, tell us about how to live so that we won't be ashamed when He returns?

Prayer Time ⫸
Use the *Our Daily Bread* article on the next page as a guide for a devotional and meditation time relating to the end times.

Reflect

We began this series of Bible lessons with the proposition that Christ is the key to end-time events (p. 9). How has this been affirmed through this study?

Take a look at Section 7: Final Thoughts. In what ways can you relate to Clair Hess and his fears as a child? After reading "What Does This Mean To Me?" on page 57, can you say for sure that you are ready for the Lord's return?

End-Time Events

I n 1947, scientists created the Doomsday Clock to symbolically show how close they believe the world is to a nuclear holocaust. In 1953, after the US tested a hydrogen bomb, the hands were set at two minutes before midnight. Since then they have been pushed back and forth thirteen times. The clock's safest setting was in 1991, after the US and Russia signed an arms-reduction treaty. The time was then set at seventeen minutes before midnight. But in May 1999, after India and Pakistan set off nuclear blasts, the hands were advanced to 11:51. In early 2012, the clock was reset to five minutes before midnight.

God has a "clock" too. Over the centuries, prophecy buffs have tried to "set the hands" by predicting the "midnight hour" of Christ's return. But their date-settings have failed and left many people disillusioned. Conflicting views of the precise order of events and the nearness of His coming have diverted many from our Lord's primary reason for speaking about these events. He didn't want prophecy to become a divisive battleground, but a unifying truth for believers.

When Jesus spoke of His return, it was to remind us to "be ready" (Matthew 24:44). We are to be faithfully serving Him (v. 45) by faithfully serving the needs of others. Let's leave the hands of God's clock in His hands.

—*Dennis De Haan*

MATTHEW 24:44—

Be ready, for the Son of Man is coming at an hour you do not expect.

■ Read today's *Our Daily Bread* at **www.rbc.org/odb**

Final Thoughts:
What Does This Mean?

"My Life Was Turned Around"

Clair Hess, retired senior editor of RBC Ministries, tells how his fear of the second coming of Christ was changed to joyful expectation through a correct understanding of the Bible teaching about end-time events.

One of the memories of my childhood and teen years is not pleasant; in fact, it is a recollection of fear. I remember actually trembling at the thought that the "end of the world" might be near.

I don't recall hearing much teaching as a boy about the rapture, the glorious appearing of Christ, or the millennium. Instead, the people I worshiped with placed an emphasis on the earth burning up with great heat, the sun being darkened, and the moon turning to blood. These images seared my mind with fear, dimmed my interest in the second coming, and drained any assurance I had that Christ would protect His own from the coming tribulation.

When I did hear a message about the Lord's return, I was afraid that I would be left behind. I came home one day after school and found no one there. I was petrified! I was sure that the Lord had come and that I was the only one in my family who was left to face the horrors of the end of time. I had not been taught that because I had received Christ as my Savior I was really safe—for time and eternity.

Although I knew that heaven is the final home of the Christian (and surely everyone wanted to go there, not to the other place), it seemed that only old people spoke of it.

No one was really in any hurry to get there. Songs portrayed the beauties and wonders of the "home over there," but they were sung most often at funerals. I was secretly hoping that Jesus would not come in my lifetime. I had too much I wanted to do. Living seemed more precious, more exciting, than being with Jesus.

After high school, I became interested in the Bible teaching I heard on the radio. I began attending summer gospel tent meetings. I bought a study Bible, and I started reading it with friends. An uncle helped me to understand the sequence of coming events in prophecy. My fears vanished as I read Titus 2:13, "Looking for the blessed hope and glorious appearing of our great God and Savior Jesus Christ."

I learned to live each day in the sure promise of John 14:1–3, where Jesus told us not to be troubled, that He is preparing a place for us, and that He will come back to take us to be with Him. As I've grown older, some of my loved ones and friends have been called to their heavenly home. They have gone to be "with Christ, which is far better" (Philippians 1:23). I know the Lord more intimately now, and heaven seems much closer than it did before. I would be glad if He came today.

Christ, who loved me and gave himself for me, is coming. It may be today! Life is more exhilarating now. Each day is an adventure. Yes, an understanding of God's program for the future has turned my life around.

What Does This Mean To Me?

We have answered the question, "What can we know about the end times?" Using the Bible as our guide, we have surveyed what God has revealed about the end of this age and the ages to come. We have looked in on scenes of indescribable bloodshed, horror, and death. And we have had a glimpse of bliss and goodness that surpasses human comprehension.

If you have trusted in Christ as your Lord and Savior, you can have confidence about the future. A day is coming, perhaps soon, when the Lord will return for you. Then you will return with Christ to share in His millennial rule. And after the thousand years are over, you will live with Him in a new world forever in a life of happiness and fulfillment that centers on the Lord Jesus.

But if you are not a Christian, the future is not so promising. The wrath of God will be poured out on the earth, and on you, in a time of terrible war, disease, and famine. And beyond that lies the second death—a fate every bit as real for the unbeliever as heaven is for the person who trusts in Christ.

The countdown continues. The time of opportunity is now. Make your decision. Trust Christ today. Believing that He died to pay the penalty for your sins, ask Him to save you. He has promised that He would. Then, when you have done so, your future will be secure—both in this life and in the ages to come.

● LEADER'S and USER'S GUIDE

Overview of Lessons

STUDY	TOPIC	BIBLE TEXT	READING	QUESTIONS
1	Setting the Stage	John 14:1–3	pp. 6–9	pp. 10–11
2	Christ's Return in the Air	1 Thessalonians 4:16–18	pp. 13–17	pp. 18–19
3	Antichrist and Trouble	2 Thessalonians 2:3–8	pp. 21–25	pp. 26–27
4	The Second Coming/Millennium	Revelation 20:4–6	pp. 29–33	pp. 34–35
5	Judgment for Unbelievers	Revelation 21:1–4	pp. 37–41	pp. 42–43
6	Considering the Facts	1 John 3:1–3	pp. 45–50	pp. 52–53

Pulpit Sermon Series (for pastors and church leaders)

Although the Discovery Series Bible Study is primarily for personal and group study, pastors may want to use this material as the foundation for a series of messages on this important issue. The suggested topics and their corresponding texts from the Overview of Lessons above can be used as an outline for a sermon series.

DSBS User's Guide (for individuals and small groups)

Individuals—Personal Study

• Read the designated pages of the book.

• Carefully consider the study questions, and write out answers for each.

Small Groups—Bible-Study Discussion

• To maximize the value of the time spent together, each member should do the lesson work prior to the group meeting.

• Recommended discussion time: 45 minutes.

• Engage the group in a discussion of the questions—seeking full participation from each member.

Note To The Reader

The publisher invites you to share your response to the message of this book by writing Discovery House Publishers, P.O. Box 3566, Grand Rapids, MI 49501, USA. For information about other Discovery House books, music, videos, or DVDs, contact us at the same address or call 1–800–653–8333. Find us on the Internet at **http://www.dhp.org/** or send e-mail to **books@dhp.org**.